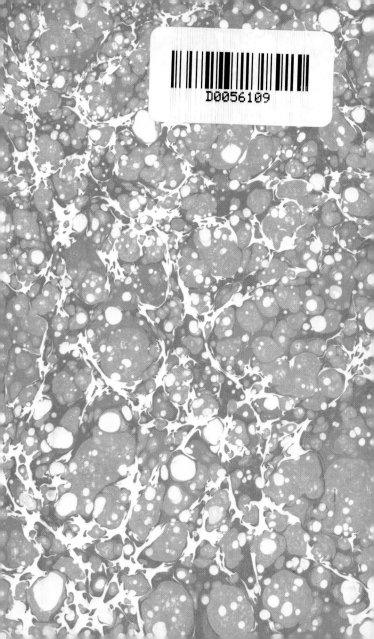

GREAT IRISH POETS

GREAT IRISH POETS

W. B. Yeats
THE LAST ROMANTIC

❀❀❀❀❀❀❀❀❀❀❀❀❀❀❀❀❀❀❀❀❀❀❀

Edited and with an introduction
by Peter Porter

Clarkson N. Potter, Inc./Publishers NEW YORK

Published in the United States by Clarkson N. Potter, Inc.,
201 East 50th Street, New York, New York 10022
and distributed by Crown Publishers, Inc.
Published in Great Britain by Aurum Press Ltd,
33 Museum Street, London WC1A 1LD, England

CLARKSON N. POTTER, POTTER, THE GREAT POETS,
and colophon are trademarks of Clarkson N. Potter, Inc.

Picture research by Juliet Brightmore

Manufactured in Hong Kong

Library of Congress Cataloging-in-Publication Data

Yeats, W. B. (William Butler), 1865–1939
Great Irish poets.   W. B. Yeats, the last romantic/edited and
with an introduction by Peter Porter.
p.   cm. — (Great poets series)
Includes bibliographical references.
ISBN 0–517–57379–2 : $8.95
I. Porter, Peter. II. Title. III. Title: W. B. Yeats, the last
romantic. IV. Series.
PR5902.P67   1989   89–25509
621'.8—dc20

10 9 8 7 6 5 4 3 2 1
First Edition

CONTENTS

INTRODUCTION

W. B. Yeats has long been regarded as the most striking example of a late developer, a poet who created his greatest masterpieces at the end of his life. In other arts, such a late flowering might not be considered unusual, but poets are expected to be precocious, flame briefly and die young. Most did nothing of the sort, but the example of the English Romantics – Keats, Shelley and Byron – all of whom died prematurely, makes Yeats's career an especially interesting one. For Yeats was beyond doubt an unrepentant Romantic in his temperament, his life and his poetry. But he lived on into an unromantic and sceptical era, duly adapting his style to the altered needs of the twentieth century, especially after the First World War. Modern taste admires him for purging his verse of the vaguenesses of Romanticism and points to his genius at forging a prophetic voice for a violent epoch. In doing so, however, it runs the risk of underestimating the earlier lyrical poetry. 'We were the last romantics,' Yeats wrote of his friends and fellow-poets of the *fin de siècle* 1890s, and the spirit of Romanticism persisted in his poetry to the end of his life.

Confronted by this 'dual' attitude – looking back to Tennyson and Victorian sensuousness and forward to modern hardness of edge and acerbity – readers and commentators have tended to concentrate on the later Yeats. But there are great rewards to be had from the work of the earlier and more overtly romantic writer. The exceedingly handsome young poet – some of his good looks are still on view in the Augustus John portrait of 1907 – was happy to join the fraternity of

Romantics and Aesthetes of the 1890s, to be friend and colleague of Lionel Johnson and Ernest Dowson, as well as fascinated observer of fellow-countryman Oscar Wilde. Perhaps, though, his lineal descent was from the English Pre-Raphaelites and Swinburne. In Dublin, he became the focus of the new Irish Nationalist movement. Themes from Irish legend inspire a number of his earliest poems – Fergus, Cuchulain, Deirdre and other heroes and heroines from *The Tain* and its companion epics adorn his verse. Only later did the myths of Ireland give way in his work to the agonies of political struggle. And there is always the haunted Irish landscape as backdrop to his passionate interest in human love and the ravages of time. 'Romantic Ireland's dead and gone/It's with O'Leary in the grave,' he wrote in 'September 1913', but Romantic Ireland goes on living in his poetry.

Yeats was fortunate, in a literary sense, in being born an Irishman. The Industrial Revolution scarcely affected Ireland, whatever miseries her subjugation to the English Crown and English absentee landlords brought upon the Irish people. Yeats, like his diametric opposite, Bernard Shaw, spoke and wrote a pre-industrial English: the language of Swift and Goldsmith proved, in his hands, to be a clearer and more subtle instrument than mainland English could be by the time he began to write. There is a clarity of structure, a freshness of utterance in his voice which helps sustain the romantic subjects he espouses. Like Wordsworth, he believed that poetry is nothing less than 'the true voice of feeling'.

William Butler Yeats was born in the middle-class suburb of Sandymount on the shores of Dublin Bay in 1865. He belonged, as have so many great Irish writers, to the ranks of the Irish Protestants, known generally as the Anglo-Irish Ascendancy. From Swift onwards, through Wolfe Tone and Parnell (whom Yeats was to make one of his cherished characters or 'masks'), these men and women have proved Irish patriots and rebels against English dominance. Their rebellion has been an aristocratic one, however, and they have often made uncomfortable allies for the Nationalist Catholic majority. Yeats's friends were the owners of the great country houses of Ireland, and the professional men and women and artists of Dublin. Yet he never lost touch with the non-literary inhabitants of his country – whether he was thinking of 'the hard-riding country gentlemen', the 'indomitable Irishry' or of 'roads full of beggars', he saw Ireland in its entirety and celebrated it as a land of mystic strength.

This selection is designed not just to emphasize the romanticism of Yeats's poetry, but also to link his early verse to his better-known later work by choosing poems whose themes recur throughout his career. From the simple lyricism of the well-known anthology piece, 'The Lake Isle of Innisfree' to the mature mysticism of 'The Cold Heaven', the reader can observe a mind growing ever more adept at matching intense feeling with fully crafted art. There are great love poems here – 'The Sorrow of Love' and 'No Second Troy' inspired by his life-long Muse, Maude Gonne; sophisticated ballads – 'The Happy Townland' and 'The Grey Rock'; and, always, an unmistakable individual voice. 'All things can tempt me from this craft of verse,' he apologized. In fact, nothing could divert him from his conviction that poetry is where life meets truth at the most unswervable angle.

The Sad Shepherd

There was a man whom Sorrow named his friend,
And he, of his high comrade Sorrow dreaming,
Went walking with slow steps along the gleaming
And humming sands, where windy surges wend:
And he called loudly to the stars to bend
From their pale thrones and comfort him, but they
Among themselves laugh on and sing alway:
And then the man whom Sorrow named his friend
Cried out, *Dim sea, hear my most piteous story!*
The sea swept on and cried her old cry still,
Rolling along in dreams from hill to hill.
He fled the persecution of her glory
And, in a far-off, gentle valley stopping,
Cried all his story to the dewdrops glistening.
But naught they heard, for they are always listening,
The dewdrops, for the sound of their own dropping.
And then the man whom Sorrow named his friend
Sought once again the shore, and found a shell,
And thought, *I will my heavy story tell*
Till my own words, re-echoing, shall send
Their sadness through a hollow, pearly heart;
And my own tale again for me shall sing,
And my own whispering words be comforting,
And lo! my ancient burden may depart.
Then he sang softly nigh the pearly rim;
But the sad dweller by the sea-ways lone
Changed all he sang to inarticulate moan
Among her wildering whirls, forgetting him.

Down by the Salley Gardens

Down by the salley gardens my love and I did
   meet;
She passed the salley gardens with little snow-white
   feet.
She bid me take love easy, as the leaves grow on
   the tree;
But I, being young and foolish, with her would not
   agree.

In a field by the river my love and I did stand,
And on my leaning shoulder she laid her snow-
   white hand.
She bid me take life easy, as the grass grows on the
   weirs;
But I was young and foolish, and now am full of
   tears.

The Rose of the World

Who dreamed that beauty passes like a dream?
For these red lips, with all their mournful pride,
Mournful that no new wonder may betide,
Troy passed away in one high funeral gleam,
And Usna's children died.

We and the labouring world are passing by:
Amid men's souls, that waver and give place
Like the pale waters in their wintry race,
Under the passing stars, foam of the sky,
Lives on this lonely face.

Bow down, archangels, in your dim abode:
Before you were, or any hearts to beat,
Weary and kind one lingered by His seat;
He made the world to be a grassy road
Before her wandering feet.

The Sorrow of Love

The brawling of a sparrow in the eaves,
The brilliant moon and all the milky sky,
And all that famous harmony of leaves,
Had blotted out man's image and his cry.

A girl arose that had red mournful lips
And seemed the greatness of the world in tears,
Doomed like Odysseus and the labouring ships
And proud as Priam murdered with his peers;

Arose, and on the instant clamorous eaves,
A climbing moon upon an empty sky,
And all that lamentation of the leaves,
Could but compose man's image and his cry.

The Lake Isle of Innisfree

I will arise and go now, and go to Innisfree,
And a small cabin build there, of clay and wattles
    made:
Nine bean-rows will I have there, a hive for the
    honey-bee,
And live alone in the bee-loud glade.

And I shall have some peace there, for peace comes
    dropping slow,
Dropping from the veils of the morning to where
    the cricket sings;
There midnight's all a glimmer, and noon a purple
    glow,
And evening full of the linnet's wings.

I will arise and go now, for always night and day
I hear lake water lapping with low sounds by the
    shore;
While I stand on the roadway, or on the pavements
    grey,
I hear it in the deep heart's core.

To Some I have Talked with by the Fire

While I wrought out these fitful Danaan rhymes,
My heart would brim with dreams about the times
When we bent down above the fading coals
And talked of the dark folk who live in souls
Of passionate men, like bats in the dead trees;
And of the wayward twilight companies
Who sigh with mingled sorrow and content,
Because their blossoming dreams have never bent
Under the fruit of evil and of good:
And of the embattled flaming multitude
Who rise, wing above wing, flame above flame,
And, like a storm, cry the Ineffable Name,
And with the clashing of their sword-blades make
A rapturous music, till the morning break
And the white hush end all but the loud beat
Of their long wings, the flash of their white feet.

When You Are Old

When you are old and grey and full of sleep,
And nodding by the fire, take down this book,
And slowly read, and dream of the soft look
Your eyes had once, and of their shadows deep;

How many loved your moments of glad grace,
And loved your beauty with love false or true,
But one man loved the pilgrim soul in you,
And loved the sorrows of your changing face;

And bending down beside the glowing bars,
Murmur, a little sadly, how Love fled
And paced upon the mountains overhead
And hid his face amid a crowd of stars.

The Lamentation of the Old Pensioner

Although I shelter from the rain
Under a broken tree,
My chair was nearest to the fire
In every company
That talked of love or politics,
Ere Time transfigured me.

Though lads are making pikes again
For some conspiracy,
And crazy rascals rage their fill
At human tyranny,
My contemplations are of Time
That has transfigured me.

There's not a woman turns her face
Upon a broken tree,
And yet the beauties that I loved
Are in my mmemory;
I spit into the face of Time
That has transfigured me.

The Valley of the Black Pig

The dews drop slowly and dreams gather:
    unknown spears
Suddenly hurtle before my dream-awakened eyes,
And then the clash of fallen horsemen and the
    cries
Of unknown perishing armies beat about my ears.
We who still labour by the cromlech on the shore,
The grey cairn on the hill, when day sinks drowned
    in dew,
Being weary of the world's empires, bow down to
    you,
Master of the still stars and of the flaming door.

He Wishes for the Cloths of Heaven

Had I the heavens' embroidered cloths,
Enwrought with golden and silver light,
The blue and the dim and the dark cloths
Of night and light and the half-light,
I would spread the cloths under your feet:
But I, being poor, have only my dreams;
I have spread my dreams under your feet;
Tread softly because you tread on my dreams.

Who Goes with Fergus?

Who will go drive with Fergus now,
And pierce the deep wood's woven shade,
And dance upon the level shore?
Young man, lift up your russet brow,
And lift your tender eyelids, maid,
And brood on hopes and fear no more.

And no more turn aside and brood
Upon love's bitter mystery;
For Fergus rules the brazen cars,
And rules the shadows of the wood,
And the white breast of the dim sea
And all dishevelled wandering stars.

Never Give all the Heart

Never give all the heart, for love
Will hardly seem worth thinking of
To passionate women if it seem
Certain, and they never dream
That it fades out from kiss to kiss;
For everything that's lovely is
But a brief, dreamy, kind delight.
O never give the heart outright,
For they, for all smooth lips can say,
Have given their hearts up to the play.
And who could play it well enough
If deaf and dumb and blind with love?
He that made this knows all the cost,
For he gave all his heart and lost.

The Ragged Wood

O hurry where by water among the trees
The delicate-stepping stag and his lady sigh,
When they have but looked upon their images –
Would none had ever loved but you and I!

Or have you heard that sliding silver-shoed
Pale silver-proud queen-woman of the sky,
When the sun looked out of his golden hood? –
O that none ever loved but you and I!

O hurry to the ragged wood, for there
I will drive all those lovers out and cry –
O my share of the world, O yellow hair!
No one has ever loved but you and I.

The Song of Wandering Aengus

I went out to the hazel wood,
Because a fire was in my head,
And cut and peeled a hazel wand,
And hooked a berry to a thread;
And when white moths were on the wing,
And moth-like stars were flickering out,
I dropped the berry in a stream
And caught a little silver trout.

When I had laid it on the floor
I went to blow the fire aflame,
But something rustled on the floor,
And some one called me by my name:
It had become a glimmering girl
With apple blossom in her hair
Who called me by my name and ran
And faded through the brightening air.

Though I am old with wandering
Through hollow lands and hilly lands,
I will find out where she has gone,
And kiss her lips and take her hands;
And walk among long dappled grass,
And pluck till time and times are done
The silver apples of the moon,
The golden apples of the sun.

The Folly of Being Comforted

One that is ever kind said yesterday:
'Your well-belovèd's hair has threads of grey,
And little shadows come about her eyes;
Time can but make it easier to be wise
Though now it seems impossible, and so
All that you need is patience.'

                        Heart cries, 'No,
I have not a crumb of comfort, not a grain.
Time can but make her beauty over again:
Because of that great nobleness of hers
The fire that stirs about her, when she stirs,
Burns but more clearly. O she had not these ways
When all the wild summer was in her gaze.'

O heart! O heart! if she'd but turn her head,
You'd know the folly of being comforted.

Against Unworthy Praise

O heart, be at peace, because
Nor knave nor dolt can break
What's not for their applause,
Being for a woman's sake.
Enough if the work has seemed,
So did she your strength renew,
A dream that a lion had dreamed
Till the wilderness cried aloud,
A secret between you two,
Between the proud and the proud.

What, still you would have their praise!
But here's a haughtier text,
The labyrinth of her days
That her own strangeness perplexed;
And how what her dreaming gave
Earned slander, ingratitude,
From self-same dolt and knave;
Aye, and worse wrong than these.
Yet she, singing upon her road,
Half lion, half child, is at peace.

The Fiddler of Dooney

When I play on my fiddle in Dooney,
Folk dance like a wave of the sea;
My cousin is priest in Kilvarnet,
My brother in Mocharabuiee.

I passed my brother and cousin:
They read in their books of prayer;
I read in my book of songs
I bought at the Sligo fair.

When we come at the end of time
To Peter sitting in state,
He will smile on the three old spirits,
But call me first through the gate;

For the good are always the merry,
Save by an evil chance,
And the merry love the fiddle,
And the merry love to dance:

And when the folk there spy me,
They will all come up to me,
With 'Here is the fiddler of Dooney!'
And dance like a wave of the sea.

The Fascination of What's Difficult

The fascination of what's difficult
Has dried the sap out of my veins, and rent
Spontaneous joy and natural content
Out of my heart. There's something ails our colt
That must, as if it had not holy blood
Nor on Olympus leaped from cloud to cloud,
Shiver under the lash, strain, sweat and jolt
As though it dragged road-metal. My curse on plays
That have to be set up in fifty ways,
On the day's war with every knave and dolt,
Theatre business, management of men.
I swear before the dawn comes round again
I'll find the stable and pull out the bolt.

The Coming of Wisdom with Time

Though leaves are many, the root is one;
Through all the lying days of my youth
I swayed my leaves and flowers in the sun;
Now I may wither into the truth.

On hearing that the Students of our New University have joined the Agitation against Immoral Literature

Where, where but here have Pride and Truth,
That long to give themselves for wage,
To shake their wicked sides at youth
Restraining reckless middle-age?

To a Poet, who would have me Praise certain Bad Poets, Imitators of His and Mine

You say, as I have often given tongue
In praise of what another's said or sung,
'Twere politic to do the like by these;
But was there ever dog that praised his fleas?

Red Hanrahan's Song about Ireland

The old brown thorn-trees break in two high over
    Cummen Strand,
Under a bitter black wind that blows from the left
    hand;
Our courage breaks like an old tree in a black wind
    and dies,
But we have hidden in our hearts the flame out of
    the eyes
Of Cathleen, the daughter of Houlihan.

The wind has bundled up the clouds high over
    Knocknarea,
And thrown the thunder on the stones for all that
    Maeve can say.
Angers that are like noisy clouds have set our
    hearts abeat;
But we have all bent low and low and kissed the
    quiet feet
Of Cathleen, the daughter of Houlihan.

The yellow pool has overflowed high up on
    Clooth-na-Bare,
For the wet winds are blowing out of the clinging
    air;
Like heavy flooded waters our bodies and our blood;
But purer than a tall candle before the Holy Rood
Is Cathleen, the daughter of Houlihan.

The Grey Rock

Poets with whom I learned my trade,
Companions of the Cheshire Cheese,
Here's an old story I've remade,
Imagining 'twould better please
Your ears than stories now in fashion,
Though you may think I waste my breath
Pretending that there can be passion
That has more life in it than death,
And though at bottling of your wine
Old wholesome Goban had no say;
The moral's yours because it's mine.

When cups went round at close of day –
Is not that how good stories run? –
The gods were sitting at the board
In their great house at Slievenamon.
They sang a drowsy song, or snored,
For all were full of wine and meat.
The smoky torches made a glare
On metal Goban 'd hammered at,
On old deep silver rolling there
Or on some still unemptied cup
That he, when frenzy stirred his thews,
Had hammered out on mountain top
To hold the sacred stuff he brews
That only gods may buy of him.

Now from that juice that made them wise
All those had lifted up the dim
Imaginations of their eyes,
For one that was like woman made
Before their sleepy eyelids ran
And trembling with her passion said,
'Come out and dig for a dead man,
Who's burrowing somewhere in the ground,
And mock him to his face and then
Hollo him on with horse and hound,
For he is the worst of all dead men.'

We should be dazed and terror-struck,
If we but saw in dreams that room,
Those wine-drenched eyes, and curse our luck
That emptied all our days to come.
I knew a woman none could please,
Because she dreamed when but a child
Of men and women made like these;
And after, when her blood ran wild,
Had ravelled her own story out,
And said, 'In two or in three years
I needs must marry some poor lout,'
And having said it, burst in tears.

Since, tavern comrades, you have died,
Maybe your images have stood,
Mere bone and muscle thrown aside,
Before that roomful or as good.
You had to face your ends when young –
'Twas wine or women, or some curse –
But never made a poorer song
That you might have a heavier purse,
Nor gave loud service to a cause
That you might have a troop of friends.
You kept the Muses' sterner laws,
And unrepenting faced your ends,
And therefore earned the right – and yet
Dowson and Johnson most I praise –
To troop with those the world's forgot,
And copy their proud steady gaze.

'The Danish troop was driven out
Between the dawn and dusk,' she said;
'Although the event was long in doubt,
Although the King of Ireland's dead
And half the kings, before sundown
All was accomplished.

    'When this day
Murrough, the King of Ireland's son,
Foot after foot was giving way,
He and his best troops back to back

Had perished there, but the Danes ran,
Stricken with panic from the attack,
The shouting of an unseen man;
And being thankful Murrough found,
Led by a footsole dipped in blood
That had made prints upon the ground,
Where by old thorn-trees that man stood;
And though when he gazed here and there,
He had but gazed on thorn-trees, spoke,
"Who is the friend that seems but air
And yet could give so fine a stroke?"
Thereon a young man met his eye,
Who said, "Because she held me in
Her love, and would not have me die,
Rock-nurtured Aoife took a pin,
And pushing it into my shirt,
Promised that for a pin's sake
No man should see to do me hurt;
But there it's gone; I will not take
The fortune that had been my shame
Seeing, King's son, what wounds you have."
'Twas roundly spoke, but when night came
He had betrayed me to his grave,
For he and the King's son were dead.
I'd promised him two hundred years,
And when for all I'd done or said –
And these immortal eyes shed tears –
He claimed his country's need was most,
I'd saved his life, yet for the sake
Of a new friend he has turned a ghost.

What does he care if my heart break?
I call for spade and horse and hound
That we may harry him.' Thereon
She cast herself upon the ground
And rent her clothes and made her moan:
'Why are they faithless when their might
Is from the holy shades that rove
The grey rock and the windy light?
Why should the faithfullest heart most love
The bitter sweetness of false faces?
Why must the lasting love what passes,
Why are the gods by men betrayed?

But thereon every god stood up
With a slow smile and without sound,
And stretching forth his arm and cup
To where she moaned upon the ground,
Suddenly drenched her to the skin;
And she with Goban's wine adrip,
No more remembering what had been,
Stared at the gods with laughing lip.

I have kept my faith, though faith was tried,
To that rock-born, rock-wandering foot,
And the world's altered since you died,
And I am in no good repute
With the loud host before the sea,
That think sword-strokes were better meant
Than lover's music – let that be,
So that the wandering foot's content.

No Second Troy

Why should I blame her that she filled my days
With misery, or that she would of late
Have taught to ignorant men most violent ways,
Or hurled the little streets upon the great,
Had they but courage equal to desire?
What could have made her peaceful with a mind
That nobleness made simple as a fire,
With beauty like a tightened bow, a kind
That is not natural in an age like this,
Being high and solitary and most stern?
Why, what could she have done, being what she is?
Was there another Troy for her to burn?

The Happy Townland

There's many a strong farmer
Whose heart would break in two,
If he could see the townland
That we are riding to;
Boughs have their fruit and blossom
At all times of the year;
Rivers are running over
With red beer and brown beer.
An old man plays the bagpipes
In a golden and silver wood;
Queens, their eyes blue like the ice,
Are dancing in a crowd.

The little fox he murmured,
'O what of the world's bane?'
The sun was laughing sweetly,
The moon plucked at my rein;
But the little red fox murmured,
'O do not pluck at his rein,
He is riding to the townland
That is the world's bane.'

When their hearts are so high
That they would come to blows,
They unhook their heavy swords
From golden and silver boughs;
But all that are killed in battle
Awaken to life again.
It is lucky that their story
Is not known among men,
For O, the strong farmers
That would let the spade lie,
Their hearts would be like a cup
That somebody had drunk dry.

The little fox he murmured,
'O what of the world's bane?'
The sun was laughing sweetly,
The moon plucked at my rein;
But the little red fox murmured,
'O do not pluck at his rein,
He is riding to the townland
That is the world's bane.'

Michael will unhook his trumpet
From a bough overhead,
And blow a little noise
When the supper has been spread.
Gabriel will come from the water
With a fish-tail, and talk
Of wonders that have happened
On wet roads where men walk,
And lift up an old horn
Of hammered silver, and drink
Till he has fallen asleep
Upon the starry brink.

The little fox he murmured,
'O what of the world's bane?'
The sun was laughing sweetly,
The moon plucked at my rein;
But the little red fox murmured,
'O do not pluck at his rein,
He is riding to the townland
That is the world's bane.'

All Things can Tempt me

All things can tempt me from this craft of verse:
One time it was a woman's face, or worse –
The seeming needs of my fool-driven land;
Now nothing but comes readier to the hand
Than this accustomed toil. When I was young,
I had not given a penny for a song
Did not the poet sing it with such airs
That one believed he had a sword upstairs;
Yet would be now, could I but have my wish,
Colder and dumber and deafer than a fish.

On those that hated 'The Playboy of the Western World', 1907

Once, when midnight smote the air,
Eunuchs ran through Hell and met
On every crowded street to stare
Upon great Juan riding by:
Even like these to rail and sweat
Staring upon his sinewy thigh.

September 1913

What need you, being come to sense,
But fumble in a greasy till
And add the halfpence to the pence
And prayer to shivering prayer, until
You have dried the marrow from the bone?
For men were born to pray and save:
Romantic Ireland's dead and gone,
It's with O'Leary in the grave.

Yet they were of a different kind,
The names that stilled your childish play,
They have gone about the world like wind,
But little time had they to pray
For whom the hangman's rope was spun,
And what, God help us, could they save?
Romantic Ireland's dead and gone,
It's with O'Leary in the grave.

Was it for this the wild geese spread
The grey wing upon every tide;
For this that all that blood was shed,
For this Edward Fitzgerald died,
And Robert Emmet and Wolfe Tone,
All that delirium of the brave?
Romantic Ireland's dead and gone,
It's with O'Leary in the grave.

Yet could we turn the years again,
And call those exiles as they were
In all their loneliness and pain,
You'd cry, 'Some woman's yellow hair
Has maddened every mother's son':
They weighed so lightly what they gave.
But let them be, they're dead and gone,
They're with O'Leary in the grave.

Running to Paradise

As I came over Windy Gap
They threw a halfpenny into my cap,
For I am running to Paradise;
And all that I need do is to wish
And somebody puts his hand in the dish
To throw me a bit of salted fish:
And there the king is but as the beggar.

My brother Mourteen is worn out
With skelping his big brawling lout,
And I am running to Paradise;
A poor life, do what he can,
And though he keep a dog and a gun,
A serving-maid and a serving-man:
And there the king is but as the beggar.

Poor men have grown to be rich men,
And rich men grown to be poor again,
And I am running to Paradise;
And many a darling wit's grown dull
That tossed a bare heel when at school,
Now it has filled an old sock full:
And there the king is but as the beggar.

The wind is old and still at play
While I must hurry upon my way
For I am running to Paradise;
Yet never have I lit on a friend
To take my fancy like the wind
That nobody can buy or bind:
And there the king is but as the beggar.

Friends

Now must I these three praise –
Three women that have wrought
What joy is in my days:
One because no thought,
Nor those unpassing cares,
No, not in these fifteen
Many-times-troubled years,
Could ever come between
Mind and delighted mind;
And one because her hand
Had strength that could unbind
What none can understand,
What none can have and thrive,
Youth's dreamy load, till she
So changed me that I live
Labouring in ecstasy.
And what of her that took
All till my youth was gone
With scarce a pitying look?
How could I praise that one?
When day begins to break
I count my good and bad,
Being wakeful for her sake,
Remembering what she had,
What eagle look still shows,
While up from my heart's root
So great a sweetness flows
I shake from head to foot.

The Cold Heaven

Suddenly I saw the cold and rook-delighting
    heaven
That seemed as though ice burned and was but the
    more ice,
And thereupon imagination and heart were driven
So wild that every casual thought of that and this
Vanished, and left but memories, that should be
    out of season
With the hot blood of youth, of love crossed long
    ago;
And I took all the blame out of all sense and
    reason,
Until I cried and trembled and rocked to and fro,
Riddled with light. Ah! when the ghost begins to
    quicken,
Confusion of the death-bed over, is it sent
Out naked on the roads, as the books say, and
    stricken
By the injustice of the skies for punishment?

The Magi

Now as at all times I can see in the mind's eye,
In their stiff, painted clothes, the pale unsatisfied
    ones
Appear and disappear in the blue depth of the sky
With all their ancient faces like rain-beaten stones,
And all their helms of silver hovering side by side,
And all their eyes still fixed, hoping to find once
    more,
Being by Calvary's turbulence unsatisfied,
The uncontrollable mystery on the bestial floor.

NOTES ON THE PICTURES

p.6 *The Man from Aranmore*, 1905, by Jack B. Yeats (1871–1957). Reproduced by courtesy of the National Gallery of Ireland, Dublin.

p.15 *The Garden of Eden*, 1900, by Hugh Goldwyn Riviere (1869–1956). Reproduced by courtesy of Guildhall Art Gallery, London. Photo: Bridgeman Art Library, London.

p.19 *On a Lake, Connemara* by Paul Henry (1876–1958). Private Collection. Photo: courtesy of the Pyms Gallery, London.

p.23 *Sunday Evening* (detail) by Sean Keating (1889–1977). Private Collection. Photo: courtesy of the Pyms Gallery, London.

p.27 *Astarte Syriaca*, 1877, by Dante Gabriel Rossetti (1828–82). Reproduced by courtesy of Manchester City Art Galleries.

p.31 *The Magic Apple Tree*, 1830, by Samuel Palmer (1805–81). Reproduced by permission of the Syndics of the Fitzwilliam Museum, Cambridge.

p.35 *The Fiddler–Self Portrait* by Maurice MacGonigal (1900–79). Private Collection. Photo: courtesy of the Pyms Gallery, London.

p.39 *Lady Lavery as Cathleen ni Houlihan* by Sir John Lavery (1856–1941). Reproduced by courtesy of the Central Bank of Ireland, Dublin.

p.43 *Sugar Loaf Mountain*, 1932, by Paul Henry (1876–1958). Private Collection. Photo: courtesy of the Pyms Gallery, London.

p.47 *Maud Gonne* by Sarah Purser (1849–1953). Reproduced by courtesy of the Hugh Lane Municipal Gallery of Modern Art, Dublin.

p.51 *The Arrival of Phadrig na pib–Paddy the Piper* (detail), 1873, by Samuel McCloy (1831–1904). Reproduced by courtesy of the Lisburn Museum, Co. Antrim.

p.55 *John O'Leary* (1830–1907), by John Butler Yeats (1839–1922). Reproduced by courtesy of the National Gallery of Ireland, Dublin.

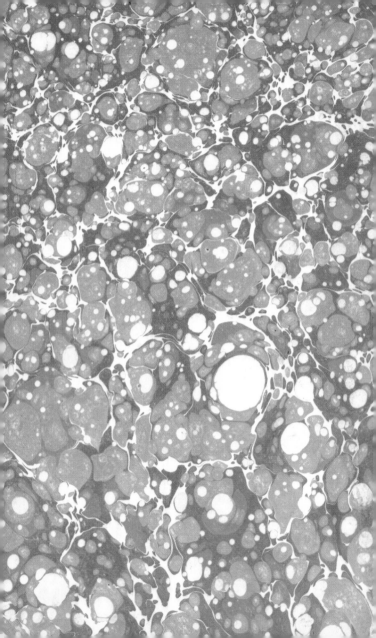